A Journey into Madness

Alistair McIntyre

chipmunkapublishing
the mental health publisher

All rights reserved, no part of this publication may be reproduced by any means, electronic, mechanical photocopying, documentary, film or in any other format without prior written permission of the publisher.

> Published by
> Chipmunkapublishing
> PO Box 6872
> Brentwood
> Essex CM13 1ZT
> United Kingdom

http://www.chipmunkapublishing.com

Copyright © Alistair McIntyre 2011

Edited by Mary Dow

Chipmunkapublishing gratefully acknowledge the support of Arts Council England.

A Journey into Madness

A story of schizophrenia

Alistair McIntyre

Author Biography

Alistair McIntyre was born in September 1964. Throughout his school education he attended 6 different schools and left at the age of fifteen in 1980. Most of his working life he was employed as a painter and decorator. He was diagnosed with schizophrenia in 1994 and had three hospital admissions because of this mental illness. He has been married twice and lives with his wife Tracey. He has a daughter Rachel from his first marriage and a granddaughter Bethany.

He is now in recovery and hoping to go back to work in mental health as a peer support worker.

Alistair McIntyre

Voices

I was working in Bedford in 1994 and decided to come home to Edinburgh. I had been feeling a bit paranoid and wanted to get back to familiar surroundings. So I decided to get a bus to Milton Keynes and from there home to Edinburgh. The bus from Bedford left at three o'clock in the afternoon so I got myself organised and made sure I was on it. Once I got to Milton Keynes I discovered there was a three hour wait until the bus left for Edinburgh, so I walked around the town wasting time. At 7:30pm I got on the bus for what I thought would be a 6 hour journey, but another journey was about to start which would last several years, a journey that was not expected but one that was to change my life forever.

It started as I was travelling from Milton Keynes to Edinburgh and had just crossed the border from England into Scotland. As the bus crossed the border I heard a voice shouting "shit, shit, piss, piss, fuck this". My first thoughts were that there was a disturbance on the bus. I stayed calm and just looked out of the window. More and more voices joined in "shit, shit, piss, piss". So I stood up and looked round the bus. To my surprise everybody was asleep. I didn't know quite what to think, but I could still hear these voices shouting. After much consideration I came to the conclusion they were the voices of spirits. Yes, that was why they called Scotland God's Country, I reasoned, because people's spirits could speak to you. This must have been the case because it happened when I crossed the border, so the location must have had something to do with it. Everybody was asleep, nobody appeared to be shouting and nobody was being disturbed by the voices; it must be spirits. This shouting continued until the bus came into Edinburgh. Then everybody started making a noise as they got off the bus and the voices stopped. I got into a taxi, went to my mum's and went to bed.

The next day I was feeling a bit paranoid but decided to go out anyway. I walked from my mum's house in Granton to Newhaven, where I used to play as a child. I wandered all round my favourite childhood haunts: the adventure play ground, the old railway and the harbour. Then I went into one of the local pubs for a pint. As I sat down and started drinking my pint, I couldn't help notice that when people spoke to me they seemed very angry and aggressive. This wasn't how I remembered Newhaven. I decided to drink up and leave. As I walked home a man approached me and asked me the time. The way he spoke made me think he was helping to keep me under surveillance in order to inflict some harm on my person. It wasn't anything he said but a feeling I got when he spoke to me. This made me suspicious of everyone I met on the road back to my mum's house. All the way along the road my senses were very alert. I noticed the slightest movement or the faintest sound and was relieved when I reached my destination.

Later that night in my mum's house, when everyone had gone to bed, I felt a presence and assumed the spirits were back. So I lay on the floor to welcome them and hopefully listen to what they had to say, but there was only silence. After about two hours I went to get up when a voice shouted stay down. This was a scary voice and filled me with fear. Then loads of voices started shouting abusive things at me, calling me all sorts of names and accusing me of things I hadn't done. Then one voice shouted above the rest "gut him like a fish!" This made me jump to my feet terrified. A gentle voice then spoke and said "we're only trying to initiate you". I calmed down and lay on the floor again expecting to be initiated, but the voices just laughed. Then I went to my bed and fell asleep.

On the following day, Wednesday, I got up really early, after about three hours sleep. It was still dark outside. I decided to get dressed and go out. I had always enjoyed going round graveyards and reading the headstones and decided that was what I was going to do that day. I walked up to the cemetery at Crew Road, past the Western General Hospital. As soon as I had entered the gates I heard a familiar voice, that of a friend I hadn't seen in a long time; he clearly said "Do you want to play spirits?" I looked round and laughed. I didn't expect to see anybody there because by now I had come to recognize the difference between the voices of people who were there and the voices of spirits and this was definitely a spirit's voice. "Good one" I thought, to which the spirit answered "woooo". This I found very funny and I laughed aloud. I also realised I didn't need to talk to these spirits but could think things and they could hear me.

I started work the following Monday and everyday I heard more and more voices, sometimes they were friendly or funny and sometimes they were angry, accusing and frightening. The voices also became more frequent as the weeks went on. I then began to think I had been chosen by God to hear spiritual things. I began to have less and less to do with people and became more and more consumed with these spirits. People, I began to believe, were out to do me harm and they always seemed aggressive and threatening. The voices were also telling me that they were conspiring against me because they were jealous of my spiritual gift. I had begun to trust the voices; I had also learnt to fear others.

Visions

After working for about five weeks I had saved up enough money to pay for a bed-sit. I viewed several and eventually found one in a respectable and quiet house in Broughton Street. I thought immediately that I could be happy here, so I moved in right away.

I was still hearing voices but began to notice something else as I watched the television and listened to the radio. Sometimes the people on the television and radio would be speaking to me personally. This was a novelty at first and it got me quite excited. I couldn't believe it: the T.V. and radio giving me messages. These messages were pleasant at first but as the months passed they changed and left me feeling responsible for the disasters I heard about on the news programs. So I stopped watching television and listening to the radio and started going to the pub instead.

I remember speaking to people in the pub, mostly women as I found men to aggressive. I soon noticed that I could tell what they were about to say or do, as if I were psychic. I then realised that they could hear my thoughts as well. This was a bit scary but fascinating. So I experimented by thinking about particular people in the pub and saying things in my thoughts. To my amassment the people seemed to react to my thoughts which confirmed my belief that I was telepathic and psychic. The problem started when I tried to switch off. Some of my thoughts were nasty and the whole pub was hearing them. I started to become scared. Maybe someone would attack me or at best someone might be nasty or start shouting at me. So I decided to leave the pub and go home.

A Journey into Madness

While walking up the road I started to calm down and relax again. When suddenly out of the corner of my eye I saw a light; this light appeared to flutter like a bird, it shot upwards and disappeared. I wondered what it was. Then a voice spoke saying "it's a soul", so I marvelled at seeing such a magnificent thing. Over the next few weeks I saw more and more souls quite often being accompanied by the voice of a spirit. One night I was walking up Leith Walk and it was nice and peaceful without much happening. I was having a great day. When suddenly out of the sky came a scream and a massive ball of light flew straight towards me, I ducked, it flew past and disappeared. A voice then spoke "that is all the souls of the people in Leith going to hell, tell them about Jesus." I felt guilty after this because I thought that I had helped condemn them.

A few days later I was watching people in the street from my bed-sit window. A particular man caught my eye. He had stopped at the bus stop and was reading the bus timetable, when all of a sudden his spirit stepped out of his body. I knew it was his spirit because it was exactly like him, same size and shape except it was transparent, I could see right through it. God has blessed me to see spiritual things as well as hear them I thought and my heart filled with joy.

I started seeing more spirits and souls as the months went by. The spirits started invading every part of my life, sometimes helping, sometimes inflicting pain on me and at times the souls and voices were tormenting me mentally. I couldn't watch T.V. or listen to the radio. I also felt responsible for the disasters on the front pages of the papers which filled me with guilt. I had a lot of periods at this time when I felt miserable but there were still moments of great joy. I was still working through all this. I didn't have much to do with my work mates though, apart from when I was warning them about hell and telling them about Jesus a result of one of my visions accompanied by voices.

Hospitalisation

After stopping listening to the radio, watching television and reading the papers, I found that I had a lot of time on my hands while in my bed-sit. So I decided to read text books on psychology. It was while I was reading one of these books I that found out about nerve endings. These give us our sense of feeling, allowing us to experience pleasure and pain. This discovery formed a question in my mind and I began to become obsessed with finding an answer. Who could I ask? I thought. Nobody I knew had any knowledge of psychology. I thought about going to a college or university but it was night time and they were closed. I needed an answer to my question and I could not wait until the morning. I had heard there were psychologists and another group of professionals with knowledge on the subject of psychology, psychiatrists, at the Royal Edinburgh Hospital, so I decided to go there that night. I walked from Broughton Street to the Royal Edinburgh Hospital in order to see a professional and obtain the answer to my question.

When I reached the hospital it was about 9p.m. and all the doors at the front of the building were closed. So I went round the side to Mackinnon House where there is an out of hours reception. There was someone on duty, a lady who said "Can I help you?" and I replied "Can I see a psychologist, as I have a question to ask them?" To this she informed me that there were only duty psychiatrists there at the moment. So I asked to see a psychiatrist. The lady then asked for my name, to which I replied "Alistair McIntyre". She then disappeared after asking me to wait a moment. About five minutes later two people, one man and one woman, appeared at the door which led into the hospital and said "Could you come with us Alistair?" They led me into a small interview room where we all sat down round a square table. I was facing the door, the lady was on my left hand side and the man was facing me with his back to the door. They introduced themselves and asked me "What is the problem?" I answered "There is no problem, I have just got a question to ask". The man replied "What is the question?" "Well" I said "are sexual pleasure and physical pain automatically connected?" At this the male psychiatrist jumped to his feet, pushing the chair back with his legs, and cried out "What sort of a question is that to ask anybody?" I simply replied "It is just a question", while wondering why he was reacting in this way. The man then said "I would like you to come into hospital for a few days". I said "okay".

I could not help thinking, as I sat with the woman and the man went to make arrangements, that this must be a joke; after all I only came in to ask a question. The man then returned and we started making our way up to Ward 3. Once there I received a medical, where they took my blood, tested my reflexes and asked me a series of questions. I was then shown to my room, which was a private room on the right hand side as you came into the ward. It was at this point I thought, maybe they need the work and that is why they have asked me to stay in hospital for a few days. I also thought I will get a few days holiday from my work. So I went to join the people in the ward in the smoking room and tried to settle in for the night.

The people in the ward all left the smoking room at about 10p.m. and started queuing in the corridor for their medication. Once they had received their medication the nurse came looking for me and found me smoking a cigarette. She had two white tablets she wanted me to take. "What are they for?" I asked. "It's what the doctor prescribed" she replied. "What are they? What side effects do they have?" I enquired. "The doctor said you were to take them." She said. "I am not taking them, there is nothing wrong with me and I don't know what they do." I said. After half an hour of trying to persuade me to take the tablets she finally gave up and I went to bed. I couldn't help thinking, while I was in bed: what do they think is wrong with me? Eventually I went to sleep.

In the morning I was woken up by another nurse offering me more tablets, which I again refused. I then got up and went to the smoking room for a cigarette. While having my cigarette I spoke to some of the patients and told them how I came to be there and how the staff kept trying to give me medication. I also told them how I was worried about the side effects and that it was strange them giving me medication when nothing was wrong with me. One of the patients, a young woman named Tracey, told me about a book called the BNF which listed all medication and side effects. She said she knew this because her step-father was a doctor. So I went into the office and asked to see a copy of the BNF. The staff asked me what I wanted it for, then refused to give me the book saying "it might get lost." I explained that I wanted to see what the tablets they kept offering me did and what side effects they had but the only thing they told me was the tablets were called Chlorpromazine.

Later that day Tracey's step-father, John, came into the hospital to see her. He had with him a copy of the BNF, which he gave to Tracey, who then showed it to me. I looked up Chlorpromazine and was horrified when I saw the side effects; I was also shocked to read that this tablet was given to people who were psychotic. I couldn't believe it: here was I, only there to make up the numbers in order to keep the doctors in work, and they were trying to get me to take tablets with horrific side effects.

A few days went past and I had not taken any medication because of the side effects. By now I had had enough and thought: they can't keep me in here when there is nothing wrong with me. I had been repeatedly told: you won't get well if you don't take the tablets. So I decided to ask for a diagnosis. I went into the office when a lady psychiatrist was there and asked for one. She said "why do you want a diagnosis?" I explained that they could not hold me there without one. She then said "That's easy; you have schizophrenia." I could not believe it. So I decided to gather as much information as possible on schizophrenia. I disagreed with the psychiatrist after reading the information but could do nothing about it. So I felt trapped and helpless and realised the only way I was going to get out now was to take the tablets which I started to do.

Moving Wards

After being in hospital for five days and not seeing anybody I knew, I decided to call my mum. She came up to see me right away. When she arrived the psychiatrist asked if he could speak with her in private. After the interview, my mum told me she had told the psychiatrist I was homeless. She then persuaded me to give her the keys to my bed-sit in order to get clean clothes for me. My mum then left the hospital, went to my bed-sit and moved all my stuff out, leaving me homeless and in hospital. My mum's words to me were "you'll get a house out of it." The psychiatrist then decided, that as I wasn't resident in the catchment area for ward 3 but was homeless, I should be moved to the ward for the catchment area of my mum's address; ward 6. So I was moved to ward 6 and instead of having a private room I was given a bed in a dormitory.

After a few days of being in ward 6 I discovered, through my conversations with the other patients, that I could leave the hospital. So I went into the office and told the staff I was discharging myself. The staff said I would have to see a doctor first, so I agreed. About half an hour later a psychiatrist appeared and took me into a room. I told him I wanted to discharge myself and he asked me a few questions about my reasons why. After answering his questions he said "you can leave if you wish." So I left immediately. I went to my mum's house that night, because I had nowhere else to go. Because I had left the hospital in such a hurry I had left my personal belongings behind. I decided to pick my stuff up the following day.

So I went back into the ward the next day. The difference this time was that I felt in control. I went to my locker, emptied it and headed for the exit. When trying to leave one of the staff said "oh, you're back in the ward." "No, I'm just picking up my stuff and leaving" I replied. I was then told I would have to see a doctor first and reluctantly I had to agree. A couple of doctors then asked me a few questions. I was then led into a room with five people in it. A woman on my right hand side started reading a sheet of paper she had in her hand saying "You are being held under the Mental Health Act Section 26", when I interrupted by saying "You can't tell me that you can read that piece of paper and I can't get out of here." "Yes I can" she said and carried on reading. I couldn't believe this, they were all serious. I was trapped, helpless and confused. The woman then finished reading, and then they opened the door, to take me back to the ward, when I saw my opportunity to escape. I was off and running, jumping down flights of stairs and tearing through corridors, being followed by a male nurse who was lagging behind. Out the side door, over the grass, straight up a stone wall and then I stopped dead. On the other side of the wall was a builder's yard. I quickly reasoned that, if I went in that yard, I'd be charged by the police for trespassing. By now the nurse was at the bottom of the wall and said with an out of breath voice "Please come down", so I did. I was taken back to the ward, the door was locked and I thought there is no chance of me getting out now.

While I was in ward 6, I met some interesting people and witnessed some strange, funny and scary events. The first person I got to know quite well was Samson. He was about 25. Quite a nice guy but had the strange habit of eating every plant that was in the ward. I remember when Samson and I were in the quiet room drawing and painting: Samson took a break. He sat in a chair next to a cheese plant and started eating it. I was a bit worried about this and said to him "That might be poisonous." He just laughed and said "It tastes great, try some." So I laughed and said "No thanks" and we then went back to drawing. By the time Samson got out of hospital he had eaten the whole cheese plant.

Then there was Roy. Roy was a bit of a loner. I remember one day he came into the dormitory when I was lying on top of my bed. He said "Hello" and went and lay on his bed. About five minutes later a nurse accompanied by a man entered the dormitory. The nurse asked Roy if he had taken a taxi from Glasgow and Roy said "Yes". The nurse then said "You haven't paid the taxi driver." "I don't need to, I'm mad" Roy said. The taxi driver, who was the man accompanying the nurse, then started shouting and saying he wasn't leaving until he got paid. Roy refused to pay the man, continually saying "I'm mad." The nurses started to gather round Roy and spent about an hour trying to persuade him to pay the taxi driver, which they eventually succeeded in doing.

A strange and frightening event that took place concerned a girl named Lucy. Lucy was a nice, friendly girl. We used to play cards while I was on my section. One day she was chatting away quite normally and we went into the corridor and sat down on the seats. We were in the corridor for a while, when suddenly she jumped to her feet, kicked in a window, fell to the floor and rolled about screaming "Get them off me." The staff came running from all directions, grabbed her, held her still and gave her an injection by force. They moved her out the ward and I never saw her again.

After completing my section and three days of close observation (when I wasn't allowed out the ward), to my delight I was released on pass for a few hours at a time. It was at this time that I was asked by Tracey (the girl who had given me a copy of the BNF) if I wanted to go to the bowling club. I remember thinking: I'm not travelling down to Granton from Morningside, where was the only bowling club I knew about. When Tracey found out that I thought the bowling club was in Granton, she informed me that there was one in the hospital grounds called the Tipperlin. Tracey and I spent a couple of hours a week in the Tipperlin Bowling Club, drinking lager. I was amazed that you were able to drink alcohol in the hospital grounds; I felt like this was a reward to the patients, for good behaviour and conforming to the hospital rules.

The Pass

After being in hospital for approximately two months, I still felt there was nothing wrong with me. I had been taking the medication and obeying all the rules. As a result, the time I was allowed out of the ward had increased from a couple of hours at a time to 9am to 9pm everyday. I took full advantage of this and only came back to the ward for food and medication at 12pm and 6pm. I felt I had to conform or be confined to the ward. It was around about this time that I was asked by the psychiatrist if I would like to go to my mum's house for the weekend on a pass. I jumped at the chance. Arrangements were made and I was about to have my first real taste of freedom for what seemed like a long time.

When I arrived at my mum's house, I thought I wouldn't have to take any tablets or obey any rules until I got back to the ward on the Sunday. My mum made sure I took my medication four times a day and I was in the house every evening, so I didn't get the freedom I expected. When everyone had gone to bed though I could do what I wanted, except leave the house. On the first night, at about 3 o'clock in the morning, I decided to make myself toast. I remember putting the bread on the grill, then suddenly feeling terrible and afraid so I crouched on the floor in the corner of the kitchen. I lost all track of time. The next thing I remember hearing was my step-dad shouting "fire, fire!" The toast had burst into flames and the smoke was belching out into the sitting room. Luckily he had gotten out of bed to go to the toilet, smelt the smoke and investigated it. The fire was put out and I was told to go to my bed, which I did.

The following day I decided to go up the town. I had heard there was an exhibition on at the National Gallery in Princess Street and told my mum I wanted to see the paintings on show. While this was true I also had another reason for going. I had painted a picture while in hospital on a large A3 peace of paper and wanted to show it to people at the exhibition because I thought it was an exceptional work of art. I got on a number 16 bus and headed for Princess Street.

When I arrived at the art gallery I was delighted to see it was busy. I went in and looked round the exhibition until I saw somebody who I thought looked like they knew a lot about art. I approached him and said "There's some really good paintings here, don't you agree?" I carried on "I'm a bit of an artist myself, in fact I've got one of my paintings here in my coat." The man then said "Can I see it?" "Certainly, I would value an opinion on it as I haven't shown it to anyone and I was thinking about exhibiting it," I said. I then took the large peace of paper I had rolled up out of my jacket and unrolled it. The man looked at it, looked at me and smiled. "What do you think?" I asked. "It's a mushroom, a big mushroom" he replied. "That's right, it's a Boletus Edulis or Cep" I said. The man then left and I went home to my mum's quite happy that the man knew what it was.

On the Sunday I decided to visit my brother, Robert, at his work, before going back to the ward. He was working in a hotel near Morningside. I arrived there at about 7pm. I wasn't feeling very good; I was hearing a lot of voices and seeing visions of spirits that were disturbing me. When I entered the bar I asked one of the staff if I could speak to Robert the chef and they said they would just fetch him. When he appeared we spoke for about five minutes and he bought me a pint. Robert then said he was very busy as it was dinner time and I was to take a seat and enjoy my pint. While I sat drinking my pint I got very confused. Everybody seemed to be talking all at once and I couldn't separate one conversation from another. Then a large Alsatian dog appeared and I watched as its spirit ate off everyone's plate, which I found very unhygienic. I then felt like the dog was going to bite me so I left without saying cheerio to my brother and went back to the ward.

Back in the Ward

A few days after my pass had finished, I was again getting used to life in the ward. Then Scott was brought in. He was a quiet guy, but used to stare a lot at me. Once he had been there a couple of days, he asked me if I had a spare cigarette. He said he would return the cigarette to me when his visitors came in to see him, so I gave him a cigarette. Half an hour later he asked me again. I didn't mind at first because I knew what it was like to go without one. However, this continued all week and I got fed up of supplying him with cigarettes and the visitors never came. So I bought him a packet of cigarette papers. I then took a paper from the packet and proceeded to make a roll up for myself from the dog ends in the ashtray (something that a lot of people did in hospital) and said to Scott "this is how you survive with no money". He looked at me a bit surprised, but made a roll up from the ashtray anyway. He continued to do this until he eventually got a visitor who brought him tobacco.

Another person who came into the ward was Helena. The only English words Helena could speak were Bosnian,coffee, good and yes. One day Tracey and I were in the quiet room when Helena came in. She smiled and said "Bosnian coffee" while beckoning us with her arm. So Tracey and I followed her and she led us to her room. In her room she had a flask, some small cups and sugar. She poured us a cup of Bosnian coffee from the flask and said "good, yes?" So we tasted the coffee and agreed it was good. We stayed in Helena's room for about two hours drinking Bosnian coffee, saying good and smiling at each other. I remember feeling like we had all had a very pleasant experience, even though we couldn't understand each other.

A Journey into Madness

Someone else who came into the ward at this time was Paul. Paul and I had some great times talking to each other. I remember speaking to him about what he wanted to do with his life. He told me he wanted to be a clown. He also told me he had dressed up in a clown's outfit and had gone about the streets of Edinburgh making people laugh. He said he had enjoyed the experience so much that he had given up university, where he had been studying to be a lawyer. This had outraged his parents and as a result they had him put in hospital. Paul insisted there was nothing wrong with him and he was going to follow his dream and become a clown. So we had a good laugh about this, then I went for a cigarette.

When I went to bed that night I spoke to Paul again. He slept in the bed next to mine and a curtain separated us, which we pulled away. We chatted for hours. Then at about 3am a group of nurses came into the dormitory, passed my bed, surrounded Paul and pulled the curtain back into position. I now couldn't see Paul, but I heard him saying "What is it?" There was no answer. Then Paul started screaming and went silent. I found out later that they had given him an injection to put him to sleep. The thought of this happening to me terrified me.

Another day on the ward, about a couple of weeks later, I was in the smoking room (as I was most of the time). It was quiet and I was enjoying my cigarette. It was nearly always quiet, before something happened. I suddenly heard someone moaning as though they were in pain. I ignored it at first, as did the nurses, but it continued. The moaning was coming from the corridor, so I went to investigate. I saw in the corridor something that shocked me. I found a woman, who had shit on the floor, and she was rolling around in it. Immediately I reported it to the staff. They then confined everybody to the smoking room, while they dealt with the situation. About an hour later we were allowed out the smoking room and things on the ward were back to normal.

Being Discharged

After being in the ward for what seemed like a very long time, I was starting to notice improvements in my mental health because of the medication. I was now able to recognize that I had a mental illness and that a lot of the things I had experienced were not real. The voices and visions had stopped, the delusions had gone and I was feeling pretty good about myself once again.

I was still having regular meetings with the psychiatrists, which I experienced all during my time in hospital. Now the psychiatrists had called a meeting which was to include my mum and step-dad. This meeting was to discuss my immediate future. The first thing I remember was, that instead of taking tablets, as I had been doing, the consultant psychiatrist said she would like me to go on an injection once a week. I said "No." Then my step-dad piped up and said "I think it would be better if you had an injection." The two psychiatrists then joined in and started giving me reasons why they thought an injection was the way to move forward. I began to feel pressured into going along with what was being suggested. As this trio of my step-dad and psychiatrists went on, I felt the pressure build up until I exploded. "No fucking way" I shouted. I then looked at my step-dad and said "You have an injection." The room went silent. After a couple of minutes one of the psychiatrists broke the silence and said "You will have to keep taking the tablets then." "For how long?" I enquired. I was told that I would have to take them for the rest of my life as there was no cure for schizophrenia; it could only be controlled by medication. The next thing I remember being discussed was where I was going to live. The psychiatrists wanted me to live in a hostel for people who had a mental illness. I refused point blank. I said

"I'm going back to work when I get out of here and I'm not staying in a hostel." They seemed quite surprised at this and said "We'll have to change your medication then. Pimozide would be best as you only take one tablet a day, but the dosage won't be the equivalent to what you are taking now." I agreed to take this drug, the meeting ended and I went back to the ward.

The following day I was taken by a nurse downstairs to an examination room. When I was in this room a woman asked me to strip to the waist, which I did. She then placed these little sticky suckers, with wires coming out of them and connected to a machine, around the area of my chest where my heart is. When I asked what she was doing she said that this was a cardiograph and it was to see if my heart was healthy. I then asked why I needed a cardiograph and was informed that it was because of my new medication. I remember thinking: I won't be taking those tablets for long, not if I have to go through all this before I can take them. So the woman did the test and said my heart was healthy. I got dressed and left.

After the examination I went to the welfare office in the hospital where I had an appointment. I was sat down on a chair and it was explained to me that because I was homeless I would need to fill in an application for a council house. I was then asked the questions on the form and the woman filled in the answers for me. At the end of the interview I signed the form and she told me she would send it away and hopefully it wouldn't take too long to get a house. I thanked her and went back to the ward.

A few weeks later I asked the staff if I could go back to work. I was told I could. So I started going to work from the hospital. I would get up at 6 a.m. in the morning, have some cereal and wait on the door being opened so I could go to work. Coincidentally Tracey started going back to work from the hospital at the same time and we used to have a laugh while waiting in the corridor. It was at this time I was told that if I was working from the hospital I would have to pay for my board. However, I only did it for a week and was discharged at the weekend to my mum's house, so it didn't cost me anything.

I had stayed at my mum's house for approximately two weeks when a letter came through the door offering me a house. I was quite excited when I saw the letter but when I read the address of the house my heart sank. It was in a part of Leith that I knew was really rough. My mum said "You'll like, it having your own place", and I felt she was putting pressure on me to take the house. However, upon reading the letter again I discovered, to my delight, that the viewing date had passed and I had missed the house because the letter had come via the Royal Edinburgh Hospital. About another week later another letter came with another offer of a house. This time the viewing date was in a couple of days' time. The address was 80/5 Sleigh Drive. When I viewed it I thought: this is great, a lick of paint and a bit furniture and it will be perfect. I accepted it and as soon as I was given a moving in date I signed the lease and moved in.

So five and a half months after my hospital admission I was now free. The first thing I did with this new found freedom was cut off all connections with the medical profession. I stopped taking the tablets and felt my life was now my own, I was the one making the decisions, whether right or wrong it was my choice and I loved it.

The Next Year

In the following months I enjoyed my freedom to the fullest. I started seeing my friends again. We would sit in each others' houses in the evenings, chatting about the things guys talk about, generally having a laugh and listening to music. At the weekend we would go to the pub. Occasionally after having a few drinks in the pub we would go onto a club. Sometimes if I had a date, I would go for a meal and then to the pictures, but only if there was a good movie showing. I worked hard and played hard. Life was great and I thought my journey into madness was over.

Then about seven months after stopping the medication the voices started again. When this happened my immediate thoughts were, is this normal or is it part of an illness. I began to reason; this happens to everybody when they reach a certain age but no one talks about it, it is part of growing up. I did not seek any help because of this reasoning but decided to keep it under control. Keeping control was really easy at this stage. The next thing that started happening was I started sensing spirits all around me, until one day at my work, I noticed the spirits were controlling me. In fact I began to believe I could do nothing without them. Spirits had been controlling me all my life, I reasoned. Before I had been unconscious of this but now I had become awakened to this fact. I felt useless, like some spirits' puppet, but I carried on thinking I was normal.

As the months rolled on the voices and spirits became worse. The voices would tell me I was being poisoned by the spirits, which I believed, because I could see the spirits putting things in my food. I remember one time I was in my mum's house and she had made my dinner.

A Journey into Madness

It was chicken, mashed potatoes and sweet corn. I was late on arriving for dinner because I had worked a little late. So I sat in the dinning room alone. When I was given the plate of food I thanked my mum and she left. I then put my arms around the plate and bowed my head, covering the plate so the spirits couldn't put anything into it. I reasoned if I lift my hands and head to get the knife and fork the spirits will poison my food. In the past few days the spirits had thrown stuff into my food making it inedible. So I ate the food with my hands, like an animal. It was the first thing I had eaten in three days. I remember thinking, as I washed my hands, if you don't learn to control these spirits you will never be a complete adult. I then went through the living room and started telling my mum that the psychiatrists did not know what they had been talking about and that there was nothing wrong with me. She said "I could have told you that. If there had been anything wrong with you it would have shown when you were a child." This made me more determined to control the spirits and voices.

I still worked all day but instead of enjoying my evenings and weekends, I endured them alone in my flat. I had stopped seeing my friends and became pretty isolated and paranoid. People once again seemed aggressive and threatening. One experience I had confirming to me that all this was normal was when I was sitting in my living room. I could hear the voices of spirits in my head. These voices started kidding me on; then suddenly they became aggressive and threatening. I stood up and said "I'm not afraid of you lot." The voices then started saying they were going to beat me up. This continued for what seemed like ages. I then said angrily "Right - meet me in the stair." There was never anyone in my stair, so this would let me know for sure if the voices were normal or not. I opened my front door, walked along the corridor and started walking down the stair, where to my astonishment I met six men. I was determined to show no fear so I walked straight at them. They walked round me and said "Hi". I immediately calmed down and felt like I had won a great victory and thought it is defiantly true- the voices are real.

It was around this time I stopped sleeping. I would try and sleep but the voices and spirits kept me awake all night. I would work all day, come home and go to bed, then lie awake until the alarm went at six in the morning. This insomnia lasted for four days. I began to think I didn't need sleep; I had been wasting my time for years sleeping when I could have been doing things. On the fourth day without sleep my mum came up to the flat. She was going to wait in my house to let council workers in while I was at work. I told her I hadn't slept and she said I wasn't to go to work. Instead I was to go back to her house and she would call the doctor to see if he could give me something to help me sleep.

When I got to my mum's house I went to bed in the spare room. Almost immediately I fell asleep. I remember being woken up by my mum who told me to come through to the living room. My G.P. was sitting there and the first thing she said to me was "I would like you to go into hospital for a few days." I then said "What you mean is if I don't go you'll have me sectioned." She said "Yes." So I agreed to go, the ambulance came and I was once again in hospital, approximately five months after the voices had started again and one year after my discharge.

Hospital again

Once in hospital I was placed in ward 3, the ward for my catchment area. On arrival in the ward I was given a medical. During this medical the staff took blood samples and the psychiatrist asked me several questions. It was during this interview that I was asked if I would take part in some tests the hospital was doing on a tablet called sulparide. It was explained to me that this was an anti-psychotic medication, and if I agreed to take part in this experiment I would be given 200 milligrams four times a day. I was also informed that I would be monitored to see if there were any side effects. So I agreed to take part in the test. I was then asked how many siblings I had and if any of them had problems with their mental health. I told the psychiatrist about my brother Ian who had had a mental breakdown but was doing fine now. I was also asked if I thought my immediate family, of brothers, sisters, mum and dad, would agree to have a blood test. The reason I was given was that the psychiatrists were trying to see if there was a connection between schizophrenia and genes. I told the psychiatrist he would have to ask my family if they would take part in these tests, which he agreed to do. The interview ended and I went back to the smoking room in the ward.

The following day my mum and sister, Carol-Ann, came up to visit me. While they were there the psychiatrist asked them if they would allow him to take a blood sample, explaining to the two of them about the tests they were doing. My mum and sister said, "If it helps Alistair we will." They were then taken away into a room where blood was taken. My mum then organised for Linda, my other sister, and my two brothers to come up and give blood, which they did. However, we were never told the results of this research. After my mum and sister had given blood we all went to the Verandah Club. The Verandah Club is a café in the hospital grounds. On the way there my sister was walking behind me. This caused me to become paranoid and anxious. I remember thinking that she had a gun, which she had gotten from her husband who was in the army, and was pointing it at my back. So I started demanding that she walk in front of me, which she eventually did. This made me feel a lot more secure. When we arrived at the Verandah Club, I ordered a coffee, which was quite enjoyable. We then went back to the ward and my mum and sister left.

About a week later I was asked to go to the welfare office in the hospital. So I went down and was informed that my employer had terminated my contract and I had to claim benefits. The welfare officer then filled in the appropriate forms for me and sent them off. This left me feeling a bit depressed.

After I had been in hospital for about a month my dad came up to see me. I remember it well; he brought me cigarettes and rather than sit on a seat in the smoking room he turned the empty bucket upside down and sat on it. He then smoked a cigarette and put it out on the tiled floor. I thought to myself when he did this; he thinks he is at his work. He was a painter and sat on tins at his work like we all did. I told him about losing my job. As usual in situations like this he was able to cheer me up with one of his stories.

That evening after my dad had left I went to the Tipperlin Bowling Club for a pint. While I was sitting in the Club I heard a voice say "Hello stranger", I looked up and saw Tracey. She said she had been bored and had popped in to see if she knew anyone. We chatted away all night, catching up on what had happened over the last year. She then asked me if I wanted to go back to her flat, which I did. When I arrived at Tracey's flat I phoned the hospital ward. I told them I was staying with a friend that night and I would see them tomorrow. They told me that I couldn't do that and was to come back to the ward, so I said "See you tomorrow" and hung up the phone. I hadn't told them where I was staying in case the police came round looking for me and took me back to the ward. We had a good laugh about the nurses' reaction on the phone. When I went back to the ward the following day nothing was said to me.

A couple of days later I was interviewed by a student psychiatrist. She asked me if I was feeling depressed or sad: A question I always answered "No" to. The reason for this was that I knew one of the treatments for depression was electro-convulsive therapy (E.C.T.). The very thought of receiving electric shocks through my brain terrified me. She then asked me if I became very happy. I said, "Not really, I'm quite stable with my mood." Then she asked me a question nobody else had asked, "Do you hear voices?" On hearing this I thought for a while, then said "I'll answer your question if you answer one of mine first?" She then enquired "What is your question?" "Do you hear voices?" I asked. She quickly replied, "I asked you first." The interview quickly broke down after that and I went back to the smoking room for a cigarette.

Approximately 6 weeks after I had been admitted the voices had stopped but instead of feeling great like the first time in hospital I was feeling pretty down. I had lost my job, was feeling a little depressed and my confidence had gone. It was at this time I was told I was going to be discharged. However, I was also told I would have to attend a day unit twice a week as part of my ongoing treatment. This unit was situated just outside the hospital grounds. So I agreed to go there as part of my treatment, then went home.

The Following Years

Once released, I attended the day unit faithfully for two months. During this time I was appointed a key worker. I always felt like the key worker was always pressurising me into doing things I didn't want to do. One activity I did enjoy though was the photography group. A group of us from the day unit used to go round places like the Royal Botanical Gardens, taking photographs. The following week we would develop the photos in a dark room; it was quite good fun. I soon got bored of the constant pressure to do activities in the day unit and eventually stopped going.

The side effects from my new medication also got me down. I couldn't sit still, my legs kept bouncing up and down and people kept commenting on it. So I stopped taking the tablets and it wasn't long before the voices were back.

However, it wasn't all doom and gloom. Tracey moved into the area, just a few streets from where I was living. Before long we were going out with each other. We would sit in our houses chatting. It was Tracey who encouraged me to seek the help of a psychiatrist, as I told her I was hearing voices. So I went along to Inchkeith House where I saw a psychiatrist, who prescribed me the tablet Respiridone. My concentration during this time was very poor. I couldn't even read a short letter without having a feeling of despair. I couldn't remember to take my tablets, so the voices got worse. Then I started seeing visions. This was all too much for me, so I told Tracey and she told me to contact the psychiatric emergency team at the Royal Edinburgh Hospital, which I did.

I was again admitted into hospital. Only this time I was placed in Ward 1, as Ward 3 was full. I remember asking one of the staff in Ward 1 whether your spirit could leave your body while you were alive. She said "Your spirit could only leave your body if you were dead." I wasn't convinced by her answer as I felt like someone had stolen my spirit. The good thing about this admission into hospital was that within two weeks, I was discharged. I did, however, have to attend Inchkeith House, where I was given a community psychiatric nurse. This nurse would meet with me once a week, to see how I was progressing. I wouldn't say much during these meetings, only that I was doing fine and still taking the medication.

A couple of years later I married Tracey. A friend took us to a place called the Castle Group. This was a drop-in service for people with mental health problems. One of the good things about it was that it wasn't connected to the health service. I had lost a lot of my social skills, but attending the Castle Group helped me regain these, as well as restore my confidence. I only went to the Castle Group for about eight months before it closed.

A new-drop in was opened in its place called Safehaven. I played a big part in starting this group up; by going to meetings with the social work department, people from the health service, the voluntary sector and representatives from the Consultation and Advocacy Promotion Services (CAPS). I now attend the existing Advisory Management Group for Safehaven, as a service user representative. Because of this involvement I was asked to join the CAPS management committee, an offer which I accepted. CAPS is an organization that empowers mental health service users to have a voice in the planning of mental health services. It is a great privilege to play a small part in this organization.

My mental health is quite good now. I still hear voices occasionally when I'm stressed. I take my tablets regularly, increasing them myself if I feel I'm becoming unwell. I have a much greater control over my mental illness than I thought possible. It took me years to get to this point in my journey into madness, but the future is looking bright. I'm a grandfather and I have a good, stable, loving relationship with my wife, Tracey. I have made many good friends at Safehaven. I also have the support of my family and friends.

Alistair McIntyre

A Journey Out Of Madness

Alistair McIntyre

A Journey Out Of Madness

This book is dedicated to my wife Tracey Jean McIntyre

Alistair McIntyre

A Journey Out Of Madness

1. Schizophrenia and I
2. Medication
3. Stigma & Discrimination
4. My Family
5. Tracey
6. The Castle Group
7. Volunteering
8. Studying
9. Fishing
10. Allotment
11. Today

Bonus writing: Poems by A. McIntyre

Alistair McIntyre

Schizophrenia and I

In 1994, during my first stay in the Royal Edinburgh Hospital, I was diagnosed with schizophrenia. I had been experiencing a lot of strange things in my life which the psychiatrists called symptoms. These strange experiences started with hearing what I thought were the voices of spirits. These voices, however, were not from dead people but people who were as alive and well as I thought I was. In fact, I even recognized several of these as the voices of friends.

The next thing I noticed was that I could see things that other people couldn't. This started with visions of souls which were bright lights that could fly. Then I began to see the spirits of living people. These were transparent replicas of them.

During these times I began to isolate myself from people. I was often frightened, lonely and depressed, but still had times of great joy and laughter. These emotions could change extremely quickly, which only made them seem much deeper than perhaps they actually were.

As schizophrenia took a hold of me guilt set in. Newspapers, television programmes and radio stations all had personal messages for me, usually pointing the finger with accusations. I thought I was being controlled by spirits, that I could speak to people by thinking words and commands, and that my own spirit was missing. In fact I believed it had been stolen and I was eternally doomed.

The people I did speak to seemed very angry and aggressive. I often walked away during a conversation with someone, which probably infuriated them. My concentration was very poor, but I still managed to work as a painter and decorator for big companies all the way through my experiences until my second stay in hospital.

I really believed these things happened to everyone at some point in their lives, like puberty; everyone had to go through it. This was just one of the many delusions that I had at these times.

Between hospital stays I had months with none of these symptoms, but they would always return. When this happened the symptoms seemed worse than before, although the stays in hospital became shorter as the tablets appeared to work more quickly.

After my third hospital admission, I had a lot of additional problems when the symptoms disappeared. I was not confident about anything. An example of this is someone wanted me to paint their sitting room door, but the thought of doing this terrified me, even though I had been a painter most of my working life. I had lost my social skills. I found it extremely hard work having short conversations with members of my family and friends. I could hardly read a short letter without a feeling of despair.

Schizophrenia had wrecked my life and I had no control over it. I had been sectioned under the mental health act at one point. I had experienced stigma and discrimination because I had this diagnosis; my life was at an all time low.

Medication

Once I was in hospital I was prescribed anti-psychotic medication. The first member of this family of drugs I became acquainted with was Chlorpromazine. I took it all through my first stay in hospital. While it did get rid of my symptoms, it also stopped me from going out in the sun for any length of time. One of the side effects was you turned orange from exposure to the sun. So if I had gone to the beach to sunbathe, I would have ended up looking like I had been 'tangoed'. Another side effect that was quite common was your joints would become stiff and difficult to move. To counteract this side effect I was prescribed Procyclidine, an antiparkinsonian. To my horror I found out after I was prescribed this that there were more side effects from antiparkinsonian drugs.

While on this medication, I went out on pass for the weekend to my mum's house. I went to the shops during one of these days and was approached by a young man who seemed to know who I was. He seemed quite friendly and engaged me in a conversation saying things like "you are just like me" and "we know the score." He then got to the point and asked me if I had any pills to sell him or score for him as he could see I was on something. I then asked "how do you mean?" I soon found out he was looking for DF118's, or Diazepam. I remember thinking this guy thinks I'm a junkie. This is an example of the social effects this drug had on me. If this guy thought I looked like I was on drugs, who else thought this and avoided me?

When I was getting ready to be discharged from my first stay in hospital my medication was changed to Pimozide. To see if I was fit enough to take this tablet I had to have a Cardiograph. As soon as I was discharged I stopped taking this tablet because I was afraid of the effect it could have on my heart. Needless to say I got ill again.

During my second stay in the Royal Edinburgh Hospital I was prescribed Sulparide. I was only in hospital for approximately six weeks this time. However, this was the start of my confidence going and my social skills failing. The side effects from this medication contributed, because of the social effects. My legs would bounce up and down when I was sitting. People kept commenting on this, saying things like "stop that, it's really annoying." This didn't help as I had no control over it, so I stopped taking these tablets and got ill again.

The fourth anti-psychotic medication I was given was Respiridone. This was prescribed by a psychiatrist from the Community Mental Health Team. However I was so confused I kept forgetting to take it. I then went into hospital where I took Respiridone and within two weeks I was discharged.

I take this medication regularly. However, it has the unpleasant side effect of making me dizzy the day after I have a drink. I do take it regularly though, and that was my first step in my journey out of madness. It was a standing joke in hospital, "keep taking the tablets," but it is so true in my case. Without taking the tablets regularly I had no hope of starting to manage my mental health.

I have quite a bit of control over the dose that I take. I started on eight milligrams a day but reduced it myself to six, then told my doctor. I still get two four milligram tablets but only take one and a half daily. This way if I feel I'm getting ill I can increase them myself, then inform my doctor, instead of having to wait for an appointment and waste valuable time.

Stigma & Discrimination

After my first stay in hospital I went back to work right away. In fact I had even started working before I was discharged. At this time I thought I could continue as if nothing had happened. I was mistaken. I didn't realise the reaction some people would have towards me having a diagnosis of schizophrenia.

When I had been ill I kept losing my bank cards. I had lost ten cards in the space of approximately six months. I had tried to get another card from the bank so I could withdraw my wages out of the cash machines outside the banks. However, my bank told me that I had reached my limit on bank cards and they were not going to give me any more. If I wanted money I had to go into the bank.

On one occasion I went into the bank for my wages and the manager approached me. He asked me if I wanted to speak to a mortgage advisor about a loan for a house. I quickly thought about it and reasoned that if I bought my house I would always have a place to stay. The manager then assured me that I had nothing to lose and stood a good chance of getting a mortgage as I was working. I agreed and was introduced to a young man who shook my hand then led me into a small office in the back of the bank. Once in the office he asked me how I was. I said "fine, but I'm just out of hospital". With a concerned and interested look on his face he asked what was wrong. I then explained I had been told I had schizophrenia. His face immediately filled with fear and he rushed me out of the office as quickly as he could, making the excuse that he had forgotten how busy he was and couldn't see me. As I left I thought 'strange', but gave him the benefit of the doubt.

The following week I went back into the bank for my wages. It was a Friday afternoon and the bank was really busy. As I walked through the bank the manager appeared from behind a glass door and stood in the door way; he put his left hand out inside the door way as if to stop people passing and said in a loud voice "Stand back, this is a dangerous man". My face went red and I couldn't help wondering what everyone in the bank thought.

One time when I was at my work I was going round talking to everyone. Then two joiners came on the building site. We started talking, but between us there were three massive rolls of carpet. During the conversation I mentioned I was just out of hospital. With a concerned look they enquired "What was wrong?". When I told them I had schizophrenia they got really angry and one of them pointed at me and cried out "come near us and we'll kick your fucking head in". I walked away shaking my head and decided there and then I was going to stop telling people I had this diagnosis because of the effect it had on people.

Another time on the same site I was painting shutters with another painter. We got talking and he was telling me about this guy that worked for the firm. As he went on he said "you must have heard of him; he's called Mad Ally". It was a big company and very few people knew everybody. He told me "he's a painter and he went to Bible College he's a right nut". At that point I thought "that's me he's talking about; that must be what they call me." I didn't let this painter know that I had been to Bible College or had a mental illness but it spoiled my day.

A Journey Out Of Madness

I wasn't taking my medication when I was working and I got ill again and ended up back in hospital. Something that happened when I was getting ill was when I worked in a private hospital. I had finished my work and was leaving the hospital. A car drew up beside me and the man driving the car asked me if I knew where Heriot Watt University was. "Yes" I answered. He explained that he was going to a lecture on human genetics and he was a doctor. "In fact I'm not doing anything, so I'll show you where it is," I told him. Then I got into the car. I started to direct the man along the road, when I suddenly realised I hadn't a clue where this university was. I decided to get him to drive me home so I gave him directions to my house. When I got out of the car I told him I couldn't remember where the University was and thanked him for the run home. I got paid off but it wasn't long until I got another job. However, they paid me off when I went into hospital.

My Family

Once out of hospital I started the process of getting access to my daughter. My ex-wife had refused me access because of my mental illness, and I had gone to see many lawyers to contest this. However, every time I left their office, within a few days I would get a letter saying, don't come back to this office or we will call the police. I could never understand why, as they always seemed fine while I was in their office. I had explained this to Tracey (a woman I met in hospital who worked in a lawyer's office) who told me, "go to my office, we can do everything legal." I took her advice but decided to ask my mum to accompany me so I couldn't be accused of doing anything wrong. My mum supported me through many meetings until the courts granted me access.

My daughter hadn't seen me for about three years at this point and she was a bit strange at first. I also had to see her at my mum's house because of the fears my ex-wife raised concerning my mental health. But I was just pleased to see my daughter again. After what seemed like a long while, I eventually got access in my own home.

During this period when I wasn't spending time with my daughter my dad would take me on painting jobs. I found this quite frightening and stressful for a long time but with his patience I got more confident. It was only the two of us working away, but I took a lot of breaks to try and relieve the stress.

My mum asked me to decorate her sitting room after I had been working with my dad one day a fortnight for a few months. My first reaction was 'no problem', but as the time drew closer to working, the pressure built up in my mind and I started to panic. I did do it though, but felt the standard of work was very poor. She didn't make any negative comments but I could see silly mistakes, ones I would normally never make. The rest of my immediate family started asking me to do jobs for them, but this only made me hate painting and decorating, a job I used to love.

I was quite lonely a lot of the time and I looked forward to my visits to my brother Robert. I would go to his house once a fortnight and have a meal. We both had an interest in drinking red wine and would buy different kinds to try them. A lot of times when I was there, I had to leave early because I got paranoid.

I would also meet my sisters at my mum's house but wouldn't say much to them because I wasn't very good at social interaction. They did persevere with me and invited me to their houses quite regularly. I saw more of my sister Carol-Ann than Linda, because my daughter was very close to her daughter Suzanne. In fact, when I had my daughter Rachel staying, I also had my niece at the same time. This kept me quite busy while they were there and helped with my recovery.

I would take my daughter Rachel and niece Suzanne to places I would not have normally gone. When they were young I would take them to the play park and the beach. Getting them home was always a problem, they never wanted to leave. This caused me a lot of stress but because it happened regularly, my ability to cope with this type of stress improved. When they got older we went to places of interest in Edinburgh that I enjoyed as much as they did.

One time we went to the Edinburgh Dungeon and as we went through we saw many things that were frightening to teenagers. In one room there was a corpse lying on a table and the staff who were dressed up as doctors performed an autopsy. At one point they squeezed some of the boils on the body and this liquid squirted all over everyone in the room, making them all scream. In another room the guide talked about the place being infested with rats; then suddenly it felt like something rushed past our feet, brushing against them as it went. My daughter and niece loved it and spoke about it for years. I must admit I thought it was great fun too.

A funny thing that happened during my access time was my daughter asked if she could have a hot individual apple pie. I told her to heat it up in the microwave cooker, which she did. However, she set the microwave oven for fifteen minutes and when the pie came out it had burnt so much it was welded to the plate. We all had a good laugh. I always checked after that how long she microwaves anything for.

When I got my house in Sleigh Drive my step dad helped me by putting some cupboards in the kitchen. He also fitted an electric hob so I could cook. However, these improvements to the kitchen caused me a lot of stress, probably because his heart wasn't in doing them. Under the hob where the oven should have gone, there was a unit, but it was too narrow for an oven. Also one of the wall units was supported by a stick that had been jammed between the work top and the under side of the wall unit. This kitchen, distressed as it was, served me well. I enjoyed many good hot meals that I would never have had, if my step dad hadn't put in the hob.

My family have been a great source of support and encouragement, and they did all they could to help me recover. However, like all families, there were times they would infuriate me and seem like they were a hindrance to my recovery, but they always acted with the best of intentions.

Tracey

I met Tracey the first time I went into the Royal Edinburgh Hospital and immediately we struck up a friendship. While in hospital she gave me a friendship bracelet which really impressed me, and we said we would always be friends. Another time in hospital she had some tobacco which she didn't like, so she asked me if I wanted it. I said, "I will have to give you something for it". She said, "Okay, give me fifty pence". I then gave her the fifty pence and she gave me the tobacco. About an hour later Tracey came back and said, "You have conned me, that tobacco is worth a lot more than fifty pence". So I gave her the tobacco back, but we didn't fall out. Later we had a good laugh about it.

Once we were both out of hospital, I met Tracey at lunch time when she was at her work. We went to McDonald's for a burger and a chat. She really understood what it was like to have a mental health problem, and I could talk to her about my experiences without being judged.

We continued meeting about once a month, and Tracey wanted us to start going out with each other. I would start a relationship, but always got cold feet and tell her "We're only friends". She put up with this for a while, then got fed up and stopped pursuing a relationship with me. She then went out on a date with someone else, which was the push I needed. I got jealous and decided to commit to a relationship.

A few times Tracey stayed at my house. One time we were there and I went to my bed. Tracey slept on the couch. She had a cigarette in the middle of the night when the light was off. When she had finished smoking she put the cigarette out. She thought there was an ashtray on the floor. When I got up in the morning there was a cigarette stubbed out on the carpet. I was not impressed. She explained that in her tiredness she had made a mistake and offered to buy me a new carpet. I told her not to worry; accidents happen. I then started staying at her house instead.

We started going out with each other in 1996 when Tracey moved into the same area that I lived in. Two years later at my sister Carol-Ann's birthday party, I asked Tracey to marry me. Her answer was "You're drunk and you'll have forgotten in the morning". But in the morning I asked her again and she said, "Yes". We were married on 16th October 1998 and it was a great day.

We go out regularly together. We never miss our anniversary and we start the celebration by playing the second song that was played at our wedding, 'What a Wonderful World,' by Louis Armstrong. Then we exchange cards and gifts, go out for a meal and have a drink. Another celebration we always observe is Valentine's Day.

Her support has been without measure; being in this relationship and marriage has probably been the biggest influence in getting my mental health managed properly. She encourages me to take my tablets regularly, and gives me the strength to try new things. She has personal experience of psychosis and can relate to many experiences I have had which the other members of my family couldn't. I love Tracey, and having someone you really love is paramount to good mental health.

The Castle Group

A few years after Tracey and I were married a friend asked me if I would go to a drop-in with him called the Castle Group. I was a bit nervous about it, but agreed to go. When we went in there were quite a lot of people there. They were doing different things. Some were playing board games, others were smoking and chatting and there were people wearing fancy dress. They were all friendly, but we didn't stay long as my friend wanted to leave. I thought at that time I needed to go to the Castle Group with someone who was a member, or be referred by a doctor or psychiatric nurse.

About a month after my first visit I went again with my friend. When I walked through the door the coordinator said, "Do you want to be a member?". I jumped at the chance and quickly answered, "Yes". This time when my friend left, I stayed behind. I sat in the smoking room having cigarettes and listening to the conversations, which I enjoyed. It wasn't long after this second visit that I began to join in the activities. I particularly enjoyed the art group on a Tuesday.

My wife Tracey began coming along with me, and with her support and the friendliness of the service users I started joining in the conversations and building my social skills.

My time at the Castle Group and what it led on to was a massive step in managing my mental health. I made a lot of friends and did a lot of things I would never have been able to do. We used to go on trips away to places once a month. One place I remember going was Deep Sea World in North Queensferry. I was amazed to see the fish swimming around as we went through the glass tunnel surrounded by the tank. We also got a behind the scenes tour and saw octopus, lobsters and many more animals that you never see in everyday life.

In the drop-in one thing we would talk about was our illness and the things we had experienced because of it, as well as ways of coping with it. Linda was a very popular person at the Castle Group and really good at giving peer support. I had discussed my illness with my wife, but now I had found a whole group of people I could talk to without getting strange looks and people rushing to get away.

After I had been at the Castle Group for about five months I was asked to sit in on a management committee meeting with a view to joining it. The Castle Group was managed by service users. I sat in on the meeting, but didn't feel I should join the management committee as my confidence, although growing, wasn't high enough for me to feel I would be competent. Also the Group was under threat of closure and I felt this would be too stressful at that time.

Two months after this meeting, the Castle Group closed. There were many rumours as to why it closed, but no real explanation was given. However, the funding was to be kept aside to start a new project, and approximately six months later another service was opened on an interim basis which we named Safehaven.

Volunteering

Once Safehaven had been going for about a month, I was asked if I would become a service user representative. I didn't think I would be any good at it, but the staff and a few of the service users persuaded me to stand for election. The election was quite a nerve-racking experience, but what a confidence boost when I was elected along with Willie and Albert.

During the first few meetings I attended I didn't say anything much, that was until I realised we were being supported by an Independent Advocacy organisation, CAPS. It was quite intimidating in these meetings with all those professionals, but CAPS staff would meet with us and find out what we wanted to say, then make sure it was heard, while encouraging us to speak. Because of this support, it wasn't long before I was raising issues myself; challenging things suggested by the professionals that people using Safehaven didn't want, as well as suggesting things they did want.

The worst meeting I was ever in was when there was only me, Willie, a couple of professionals and the chairman. The meeting started, then it was proposed that Safehaven closed within the week. We were not given any real reasons why, but before I could say anything, Willie started shouting and stormed out. I then argued that if there were any problems surely the best thing to do would be to try and sort them out as they would keep coming up in any drop-in. The chairman then made out he was ending the meeting, but as I found out from the minutes we were all recorded as agreeing to the closure of the project. In the following meeting, I insisted the minutes were changed, because as I said, I would never have agreed to the closure of a service that was so important in giving people a way of managing their mental health.

It was decided to start from scratch after Safehaven was closed and start a new service. I continued to attend these meetings and took on other roles relating to the business of setting up a new service. The Social Work Department came up with a name for the project which was The North East Edinburgh Mental Health Resource, a name I wasn't very impressed with, but had no say in its adoption. We tried to set up a management committee of service users with little success. So the social work department agreed to employ the staff. While all this was going on we lost half the funding because the commissioners felt they couldn't give us as much funding if there was no service. A coordinator was employed and it wasn't long before the drop-in was up and running again.

It was about this time I was asked if I wanted to join CAPS management committee. I agreed to come along to their next meeting. I was impressed with the committee and agreed to join. I was given an induction, where I found out that CAPS was one of the first independent advocacy organisations in Scotland and ran four services between Mid-Lothian, East Lothian and Edinburgh. These services are individual advocacy and collective advocacy. I also found out about the legal responsibilities of committee members in a charity. I was then voted on the committee.

In my first year on CAPS management committee I did a lot of listening. I was particularly impressed with the competence and confidence of Terry and Anne as they spoke at meetings. I still look up to them today. I was on a steep learning curve and there was loads to take in. I joined the committee in February and by the time the

AGM came around I was asked if I would be interested in becoming Vice Convenor, as the current Vice Convenor had to step down. I gladly took on this role and was in this office for two years. However, most of my second year I was acting Convenor as the Convenor was off sick. He did manage to be back in time for the AGM and gave his report, which I was extremely glad off. During the AGM I was voted on as Convenor. This time as acting and actual Convenor I found myself doing lots of work. This has been amazing for my confidence. I was surprised to see just how much is involved, and Terry and Anne have been a great support.

The thing I like most about CAPS is that it is governed by service users. All the management committee members are people who have had mental health problems. They also have volunteers in the individual advocacy side of the organisation who are service users, and this is encouraged. They also run projects on the collective advocacy side of the organisation that use volunteers who are also service users.

As well as my management committee role in CAPS I also interview people for the Oor Mad History project which is making an archive of the service user movement in the Lothians. I have learnt so much about the things service users have achieved from interviewing people who have been involved in the movement. I believe all this is beneficial to my mental well being.

Another volunteer role I took on was running a stress management course with the coordinator of The North East Edinburgh Mental Health Resource. We both attended a series of classes on stress management in Glasgow. With the materials we gathered we managed to tailor it to our drop-in attendees requirements. We ran it to a group of people for eight weeks and it was a great success.

Every year I had to stand for election as a service user representative. I have always been successful in getting this position. The committee was known as an advisory group, but we were working towards independence from health and social care. In 2007 we managed to get enough service users interested in joining a management committee, and we held a workshop to choose a name. The name is now SEASONS, one that we are all happy with. We drew up a constitution, with the support of CAPS and the Edinburgh Voluntary Organisations Council. We registered as a charity, and started writing policies and getting training for the skills we would need to take over the funding.

Volunteering has given structure to my life and has taken me on the main path in my journey out of madness.

Studying

It wasn't long after I started voluntary work that I started studying. The first course I did was a short Open University Openings Course. In order to do this short course I bought a computer and got someone to show me the basics of using Microsoft Word. I then applied and was accepted onto the course. When I got the materials I got to work immediately. I found that my mind was stimulated to such a degree that I couldn't sleep, so I worked all night. I had to submit three short essays for the course, and all of them were completed well before the deadlines. The fourth assignment was optional and gave you credits if you passed. I had decided to do the credited part of the course. It seemed to take forever waiting for the results, and eventually they came through. I held the envelope in my hands for what seemed like ages until I got up the courage to open it. To my delight I had passed. The confidence boost was amazing, and to celebrate Tracey took me out for a meal and a drink.

A few months later I started my second Open University Course. This was a nine month course, and if completed successfully I would gain a Certificate. Again the materials arrived and I set to work right away. All my assignments were submitted early, and I got good marks for them all. When I had passed this course I got a letter from the University telling me that I could now use the letters CERT SOC SCI (OPEN) after my name. This made me laugh, but I decided not to use them as I thought it might be a bit pretentious. It did however, do wonders for my confidence.

I then stopped studying with the Open University and started doing short courses relating to my voluntary work. The first course I did was an introductory management course which was run by Stevenson College. It was quite different doing a course with lots of other students. I felt quite intimidated at first, thinking that they would all have much more experience than me, but once I relaxed, I found them all a nice bunch of people who were willing to share their experiences as part of the learning process. I had to write a report in order to pass this course, and I chose service user involvement in SEASONS. This report helped shape some of the ways we now gather and use service user views in this organisation.

I enjoyed studying with other people so much that I started looking for other courses to do. I found that if I did short courses it was testing, but at a level that wasn't too stressful. It was also good training for my voluntary roles, and as such the organisations would pay for me to attend these courses if there was funding for training.

These courses have been good for my mind and mental well-being. They gave me other things to think about other than my symptoms of schizophrenia. Although while doing them there was an element of stress, it was greatly outweighed by the confidence boost I received upon successful completion of a course.

Fishing

It hasn't been all work and study that has helped me manage my mental health. Fishing has also been a contributory factor, or more precisely angling. I started doing this when my dad invited me to join him on a trip to a fishery called Parkley. It is just outside Linlithgow. I had been fishing with my dad as a boy, but with little success, and he persuaded me to go with the promise of catching a decent sized fish. I wasn't let down, I caught two Rainbow Trout on my first trip and I was hooked. I would go fishing with my dad every week and absolutely loved every minute of it.

We tried a few other fisheries that were just as enjoyable until we felt we should try river fishing. The first river we fished in was the Tyne at East Linton. I did not have much success there, as we were fishing for sea trout and I didn't know what I was doing. We also fished the Water of Leith where we caught brown trout and grayling.

After a few years and some time fishing in the sea for mackerel and bass I decided I wanted to learn more about sea angling. I told my dad, who said he wasn't interested in sea fishing but if I really wanted to do it I should join a club. I didn't know of any sea angling clubs but my dad suggested that I ask in the local tackle shops, which I did.

In 2004 I joined Cockenzie & Port Seaton RBL Sea Angling Club. They were all friendly people and it is quite a small club. I learnt loads from the members, and even go on fishing holidays with my friends from the club. The variation in fish species I have caught I can't even keep track of. We meet every week to discuss where we will fish, and we regularly travel all over Scotland. In 2006 I was asked if I would become treasurer of the club, which I was very pleased to accept.

Another role I took on through my fishing was peer led fishing outings for people who were interested at SEASONS. At first we would only go to places that were easily accessible by bus. The purpose was to get people out and experience catching a fish. I thought if they get half as much joy out of this as I did then it would be a great experience.

The greatest joy I got out of seeing someone from SEASONS catching a fish was when Willie caught his first fish. We had been fishing once a month for over two years. I had borrowed my dad's car to take everyone to a fishery in the hope Willie would catch his first fish of his life. I set up his tackle and we all started fishing, then Willie got a bite; the excitement he displayed was more than reward enough for the long wait. When he landed the fish he jumped up and down with a cry of satisfaction, "I've got a fish". Not only did Willie catch his first fish that day, but also his second. In fact he was the only one to catch anything that day, and he was on a high for quite some time. So at over the age of fifty Willie became a true fisherman. He told me he had eaten the fish that night and thoroughly enjoyed them.

Allotment

In 2008 I was asked to go along to the Community Flat in Piershill for a men's mental health group to talk about fishing. I enjoyed the group so much that I stayed the course. When it was finished we were told we could go to the Community Flat any time it was open. I was also informed that the local residents had applied for money to build an allotment site in the spare ground at the back of the houses at Piershill and been successful. Since I was a resident in the area I was eligible to put my name down for an allotment, which I did.

Later that year the council workers started building the allotments. They dug up a large area of ground and put a fence around it. I had been attending the Community Flat during this time, and volunteered to help mark out the plots. There were eighteen people with their names down for a plot so we decided to make twenty two plots. The reason for this was so everybody got a plot and there were four plots for the Community Flat.

The Community Flat worker Beth then tried to get a committee together to manage the allotments. So I decided to offer my skills and join the committee, which a few others also did. The first thing we did was write a constitution and choose a name. The name we chose was Piershill Plotters. Then Beth started applying for funding for us. We had to open a bank account quickly because it seemed so easy to get funding.

The allotments were then given to everyone and I, like many others, started personalising my plot. I turned over the ground and put a wooden border round it. I then placed straps of wood up the wall which made one edge of my plot. It is quite a high wall so I placed mesh over the straps and hung plant pots with herbs in them on the wall.

I didn't know anything about growing vegetables so I read a book and followed the advice that was given. In the spring of 2009 I planted as varied an amount of vegetables as I could to see what grew well in the soil, while still planning a crop rotation system. I had also planted some strawberry plants.

I went out ever week and weeded the plot and watched the plants as they started growing. They all grew well and it was great. Then the pigeons started eating my cabbages and sprouts. When I covered them with mesh the pigeons would stand on top of it and force it down so they could get to the vegetables. Eventually they stopped eating them.

The first crop I got was strawberries. They were delicious, really sweet and juicy. Then the peas were ready; when I tasted them I couldn't stop eating them. Then potatoes, and on it went. I have never really eaten a lot of fruit and vegetables, but this allotment has started to change that. Freshly grown stuff is delightful on your palate. My allotment has given me a source of fresh fruit and vegetables as well as regular exercise, two things that are good for my physical and mental health.

Today

Where am I today? Well, I have many voluntary roles, I am the convenor of CAPS, the Chairman of SEASONS and a voluntary speaker for See Me Scotland, to name but a few. For See Me the work I do is probably the final step before I look for paid employment. I go around different places such as schools and colleges, talking about mental ill health stigma and discrimination. They gave me training in public speaking and I've loved giving many talks this year. I do all the training I can, as I believe an active mind is a healthy mind. I do my fishing and work on my allotment. I take my medication regularly.

I also have a few hobbies that keep me busy such as calligraphy and mycology (which is the science of fungi) and often go around woods and fields identifying mushrooms. I also paint with watercolours and write poetry.

I have regular nights out with my friends from SEASONS. This started when we used to go out once a year for Christmas. We would have a meal and a drink. Then someone wanted us to go out to celebrate their birthday. At that time I think it was Linda and her daughter Tracey who suggested we make it a regular thing, which we did. We go for a drink, have a sing song on the karaoke and a dance. Michelle has started joining us as well; she is the only person in the crowd without a mental health issue. I often think when we are in a pub or club that there are probably more mad people in there than in the Royal Edinburgh Hospital.

My Life is really good and I enjoy it. My daughter Rachel is a mother and my granddaughter Bethany is a source of great joy. My family and friends are all there for me if I need help, but my mental health is managed so well with all these different parts playing their role that we have good times rather than crises. My rock however is Tracey my wife, without whom I doubt if I ever would have made the journey out of madness.

Cycles of Life

There is a fence around a field that never runs quite straight
Upon it hangs the gate of life that shines before dawn breaks
And in that field there stands a tree like I have never seen
Its root its branches and its bark are never ever green

One day that tree came tumbling down and life from it did spring
A spore was blown by the wind and on a branch did cling
It soon shot up, it spread its gills, and there for all to see
A mushroom that was coloured black was growing on the tree

Then came an unsuspecting man and looked on with delight
'That mushroom looks quite good,' he thought, 'I'll eat it all tonight'
He took it and he cooked it up, its sting then to reveal
The death cap that poor man had found and this was his last meal

Then laid to rest upon a hill and there for all to see
And carried there by gale of wind a seed came from a tree
The trunk shot up, the branches spread, it now stands firm and tall
It only needs to tumble down for another man to fall

I Grew a Marrow

I Raked all the ground and then planted a seed
I watered it daily and kept down the weeds
Then after two weeks it had started to show
And to my amazement a plant it did grow
The flowers appeared then they closed themselves up
The fruit then developed at incredible rates
From courgettes to marrows and then to my plate

My Mum

She's a wonderful lady she sits on her throne
She rarely complains and rarely she moans
Everyone respects her for she always cares
She has a rod of iron to rule but she's fair
She looks immaculate you can't tell her age
The grand kids all love her with them she plays
She'll be there for me and my family for good
She is my mum her name's Evelyn Wood

Bethany

She's small and she's blonde just like her mum
She plays in the park and makes it look fun
She digs in the sand and piles it high
She eats her ice cream and covers her face
She pretends she's writing all over the place
She draws funny pictures of people she's met
She'd rather have sweets than ordinary food
She sleeps all night long until out comes the sun
She is my granddaughter; I can't wait till she comes

Lochetive Midges

Sitting on my box with my rod standing proud
Surrounded by hills and very little sound
The breeze it is blowing with a cooling effect
I hear the birds singing while tending their nests

The wind it then ceases, I see one little fly
Then very quickly their numbers multiply
Soon I am slapping my face with my hands
The midges are biting but things are still grand

Then a massive cloud I can see all around my head
They're driving me mental, I start seeing red
I can't keep on fishing, I want to go home
All of my senses are starting to moan

The breeze picks back up, they all vanish again
Back to the fishing I'm now feeling sane
Where did they go to? There's not one in sight
I pray that the breeze keeps up all through the night

My First fish

I set up my line and cast my hook in
Then waited and waited most of the day
The scene it was peaceful but suddenly broken
My float started bobbing, my heart started racing

I tightened the line with a mighty hard strike
I had a fish hooked and it started to fight
It swam to the left, a sharp turn to the right
The speed it amazed me, I panicked inside

Slowly I played it until it was landed
Then into the net and onto the shore
It jumped in a frenzy and tried to break free
What it didn't know, it had been caught by me

I picked up the priest and beat it to death
I slit up its belly and empted its guts
Rapped tight in foil and baked on the fire
I had it for dinner; I fulfilled my desire

Alistair McIntyre

Love like the seasons

When love first starts it's just like spring
With new shoots of growth piercing through the snow
Birds singing and dancing for a mate
When love first starts it is great

Then love reminds me of summer days
Where young hares and lambs run and play
When flowers bloom in sun filled meadows
And nature's beauty just like yours is all around

Then autumn comes while love still flourishes
Like coloured leaves on old oak trees
Falling and floating in the breeze
Mushrooms start to have their way
And they grow strong on the decay

Then winter comes and love grows cold
By this time you could be old
No hope of seeing spring again
And in despair your life it ends

But this is only true
If you like many do
Think love is sex
Instead of something else you do

My Kitten

She's small and she's fluffy so cute you go ah
She always welcomes you when you walk in the door
She sleeps on my wife at night and by day
Fights with my hand, bites and scratches, she plays
She runs through the house like a tornado in a rage
Creates havoc in which ever room she stays
Runs up the curtains and jumps up the door
And sometimes she's peaceful and lies on the floor

Invited to the Pub

I'll have one or two is what I always say
Three or four and I want to stay
Five and six the party's in swing
Seven and eight and I start to sing
Nine and then ten I've had enough
Wake up in the morning and I'm feeling rough
'Never again' is what I always say
But I soon forget when the hangover's away
Next month's the same and the month after that
I really enjoy it but next day I'm flat
You'd think I would learn but I really have fun
So next time you're going invite me to come

www.ingramcontent.com/pod-product-compliance
Ingram Content Group UK Ltd.
Pitfield, Milton Keynes, MK11 3LW, UK
UKHW041412180426
11947UKWH00007B/97